Outstanding
OUTSIDES

HANA MACHOTKA

MORROW JUNIOR BOOKS • NEW YORK

**To Eddie,
for his constant
support and enthusiasm**

The text type is 18-point Optima.

Printed in Hong Kong by South China Printing Company (1988) Ltd.

1 2 3 4 5 6 7 8 9 10

Library of Congress Cataloging-in-Publication Data
Machotka, Hana. Outstanding outsides / by Hana Machotka ; illustrated with photographs.
p.   cm. Summary: Explores how the outside coverings of animals protect
them from enemies, the elements, germs, and drying out.
ISBN 0-688-11752-X.—ISBN 0-688-11753-8 (lib. bdg.)
1. Body covering (Anatomy)—Juvenile literature.   2. Skin—
Juvenile literature.   [1. Body covering (Anatomy)   2. Skin.
3. Animal defenses.]   I. Title.   QL941.M3   1993   591.1′858—dc20   92-19517   CIP   AC

Acknowledgments

My sincere thanks to the following individuals and organizations who made this book
possible: Bruce Lawder, director, and Karen Pankey of the Greenberg Nature Center,
Scarsdale, New York; John Lenzycki, assistant curator of animals at the Maritime Center,
Norwalk, Connecticut; Vince Hall, owner of Claws 'n' Paws Wild Animal Park, Hamlin,
Pennsylvania; Margaret Britton, for lending me her tarantula; Scott Silver of the educa-
tion department of the Bronx Zoo, New York City, for sharing his expertise; and finally
the Central Park Zoo, New York City.

Thanks also to my editor, Andrea Curley, and to art director Barbara Fitzsimmons and
designer Jean Weiss for their excellent contributions, and to my agent, Laura Blake.

Every animal's outside covering wraps around its body. It protects the animal from injury and disease and from drying out. It may also help the animal survive in other special ways. This covering can be soft, hard, slimy, hairy, scaly, or feathery.

The hedgehog's body is covered with about five thousand spines. Each spine is really a special type of hair that is as sharp as a needle. When the hedgehog feels threatened, muscles under its skin raise the spines up all over the body. An enemy that comes too close can get pricked. And if that doesn't work, the hedgehog can roll up into a prickly ball! The hedgehog's covering allows this small, shy animal to survive in its environment. As you look at the outsides in this book, see if you can figure out how each one helps the animal live in its world.

This hard skeleton belongs to a…

TARANTULA

The tarantula has no skeleton inside its body. Instead, it has a hard skeleton on the outside, called an *exoskeleton*. In order to grow, the tarantula must *molt*, or shed, its exoskeleton periodically. A split forms on one side of the exoskeleton, and then the tarantula slowly pulls its body out. Its soft body grows quickly, and in a few days the new skin hardens.

The hairs on a tarantula's body are organs of touch. If the tarantula feels threatened, it sometimes combs hairs off its body and throws them at the enemy. This may distract the enemy just long enough for the tarantula to get away.

Rough, snaggy skin belongs to a...

SHARK

This tough skin is covered with tiny, toothlike scales called *dermal denticles*, or skin teeth. They are made from the same material as the teeth in the shark's mouth. Dermal denticles are so sharp, they can scrape off your skin if you brush against them. A shark's skin is a very good shield against enemies.

Most fish do not lose their scales, but sharks do lose dermal denticles. They are always falling out and being replaced by new ones growing underneath. Dermal denticles come in different sizes, though most are too small for you to see easily. They have ridges, furrows, and points, just like regular teeth. These shapes actually seem to help the shark swim smoothly through the water.

This soft, moist skin belongs to a...

FROG

An adult frog can live both on land and in water. But it must always keep its skin wet, or it will die. The frog breathes with its lungs, but its moist skin also breathes. Breathing through the skin is very useful when the frog *hibernates*, or sleeps, underground in winter. Then its lungs stop working, but its skin doesn't.

A frog may shed its skin often as it grows. The skin splits down the belly and back, and the frog pulls it off with its mouth. Then it swallows the skin, which contains many nutrients that the frog needs.

Hard, overlapping scales belong to a...

SNAKE

Scales are hardened folds of skin. The snake's hard, horny scales protect it from enemies and keep its body from drying out, even in the desert, where some snakes live. Scales also help this animal move. The snake's belly scales press against the ground as its muscles push its body along. Clear scales cover the snake's eyes to keep them from getting dirty or scratched.

The snake has to shed its hard skin periodically in order to grow. While a new set of scales is growing underneath, the old skin starts to split around the head. The snake rubs against rocks and narrow places to help peel back the skin. By the time the snake has finished shedding, it has turned its old skin inside out like a T-shirt!

This dome-shaped shell belongs to a...

TURTLE

The shell of this box turtle is made up of hard, bony plates that are joined together. A thin layer of horny plates covers the bony ones, giving the shell its color and making it even stronger. The turtle's shell has two parts. The *plastron*, or bottom part, is flat. The top part, called the *carapace*, is domed. The dome shape makes it difficult for an enemy with powerful jaws to crush the shell.

When the turtle is threatened, it pulls its head and legs into its shell. The front and back plates of the plastron are "hinged," so when the turtle is frightened, it can close the shell up tightly like a box.

Feathers are a warm, light covering for a...

BIRD

Because feathers are strong, lightweight, warm, and waterproof, they are perfect for flying and are also useful on land and in water. The outer contour feathers help the bird fly and swim by providing a smooth outside surface. A bird keeps its feathers waterproofed by spreading oil on them with its beak. It gets the oil from a gland at the base of its tail. This grooming also "zips" together tiny barbs on the feathers, keeping the feathers smooth and close together.

An undercoat of fluffy down feathers keeps a bird warm. In fact, baby birds have only down feathers until they are old enough to fly. In cold weather a bird fluffs up its feathers to trap warm air in them. Then it may sit down over its feet to keep them warm too!

This soft, hairy covering belongs on a...

BEAR

A bear has two layers of hair. A layer of long outer hair allows water to roll off the bear's body. A layer of short underhair keeps the bear warm. A bear's hair is lightweight, so it allows the animal to get around quickly.

A polar bear's white hair helps this animal to live in its frigid Arctic environment. Each hair is translucent, allowing sunlight to go through. Each hair is also hollow and funnels the sunlight to the polar bear's black skin. The black skin warms up and holds the heat, keeping the polar bear warm even in the coldest weather. Sometimes the polar bear gets so warm, it takes a dip in the freezing water just to cool off!

We have seen that there are many different outside coverings in the animal world. Some help protect animals from enemies, the elements, and germs. Some help the animals move around. All outsides help their owners survive in their own particular environment.

Could a bird fly if it had a hedgehog's spines instead of feathers? If a bear were covered with scales like a snake, could it still move around quickly? If a frog were covered with feathers, could it hibernate underground? How does your outside help you?

An outside covering is a very special boundary between the outside world and the inside body of an animal.

DATE DUE	BORROWER
R 15 '9	CHRISTOPHER 2 4

P